SKYLIGHT

Carol Muske

Doubleday & Company, Inc., Garden City, New York, 1981

Grateful acknowledgment is given to the following magazines in which these poems originally appeared:

Antaeus: Skylight; Chivalry; Fireflies; Her Story: Leaving Eden; Ahimsa; Census
The American Poetry Review: The Painter's Daughter; Idolatry
The Antioch Review: Coral Sea, 1945
Field: Worry; Dulce lignum, dulces clavos
The Missouri Review: The Fault
Moons & Lion Tailes: Cheap Scent
The New England Review: Ransom
"The Invention of Cuisine"; "War Crimes"; and "Golden Retriever" appeared originally in *The New Yorker*.
Parnassus: Short Histories of the Sea
Pearl: Chasers
Pequod: Par; Elocution: Touch
Poetry Miscellany: Opium
Ploughshares: Coincidence; Real Estate
Slow Loris Reader: Tuesday Again
The Virginia Quarterly Review: Androgyny; Choreography
Woman Poet: Special Delivery to Curtis: The Future of the World; Chapter One

ISBN: 0-385-17087-4
Library of Congress Catalog Card Number 80–712
Copyright © 1977, 1978, 1979, 1980, 1981 by Carol Muske

I wish to thank the following organizations for their support: The MacDowell Colony, Creative Artists Public Service Program (CAPS), and The Poetry Society of America: its Alice Fay di Castagnola Award for a manuscript-in-progress. Also, thanks to my mother and father for help and support and to Barbara Trainer for her patience and editing skill.

C.M.

—for CURTIS CATHERINE INGHAM
and THOMAS LUX

CONTENTS

III

SIREN SONGS

It appeared to me
again, just after daylight,
betwixt day and skylight.

Historical Perthshire

In the name of that pure one
who could gaze till she was two.

Vallejo

SKYLIGHT

I

The Invention of Cuisine

Imagine for a moment
the still life of our meals,
meat followed by yellow cheese,
grapes pale against the blue armor of fish.

Imagine a thin woman
before bread was invented,
playing a harp of wheat in the fields.
There is a stone, and behind her
the bones of the last killed,
the black bird on her shoulder
that a century later
will fly with trained and murderous intent.

They are not very hungry
because cuisine has not yet been invented.
Nor has falconry,
nor the science of imagination.

All they have is the pure impulse to eat,
which is not enough to keep them alive
and this little moment
before the woman redeems
the sprouted seeds at her feet
and gathers the olives falling from the trees
for her recipes.

Imagine. Out in the fields
this very moment

they are rolling the apples to press,
the lamb turns in a regular aura of smoke.

See, the woman looks once behind her
before picking up the stone,
looks back once at the edible beasts,
the edible trees,
that clean digestible sky
above the white stream
where small creatures live and die
looking upon each other
as food.

Coral Sea, 1945

for MY MOTHER

My mother is walking down a path
to the beach.
She has loosened her robe,
a blood-colored peignoir,
her belly freed
from the soft restraint of silk.
In a week I will be born.

Out on a reef
a small fleet waits for the end of the world.
My mother is not afraid.
She stares at the ships,
the lifting mask of coral,
and thinks: *the world is ending*.
The sea still orchid-colored before her
and to the south the ships in their same formation

but now the reef extends itself,
the sea thrusts up its odd red branches
each bearing a skeletal blossom.
I have no desire to be born.

In the coral sea
the parrots sing in their bamboo cages
the pearls string themselves in the mouths of the oysters
it snows inside the volcano

but no one believes these things.

And these things are not believable:
not the reef feeding itself
nor the ships moving suddenly, in formation.

Nor my body burning inside hers
in the coral sea
near the reef of her lungs

where I hung in the month of December.
In the year the war ended
the world opened,
ending for me
with each slow tremor
cold
invisible as snow
falling
inside the volcano.

Worry

for SISTER JEANNE D'ARC

For some of us, they're the same,
memory and worry. At six, obsessed
with the bough in the lullaby that breaks,
I stayed awake, thinking about a cradle's
wingspan. I took the first lilacs to school

that year in a kind of gauze bunting, expecting
their necks to break before I had them in
the hands of the nun I still call John Dark.
She turned from a window where I often stood

sill-high, afraid to look over the ledge.
On the wall, Christ stood on his cross
like a man lashed to a kite. I had been
taught to believe he would hold us all up—

spreading his arms like wings across
the cracked lilies of plaster, spreading
his arms like a florist I once saw stripping
the innocent boughs for blossoms to stick
in chicken wire. *If they take your flowers,*

they might call you sweetheart, they might
catch you up with your sad bouquet and whirl

you round and round too close to the window
for comfort. Don't forget it was springtime,

when even nuns get crazy. Don't forget
though it felt like heaven on earth,
we were on the third floor.

The Painter's Daughter

It's a kind of blindness.
I'm too familiar with the style,
the images that mark his middle period.
Driving home: the road takes on
his shapes (the eyes, the cruciform fires) . . .
Always the same grove of trees
keeping his *Black Picnic:*
people eating in rows
with bones underfoot.
Could they know the brush
that drew sparks on every surface,
that picked them out like familiar stars in the dark?

Never mind the white lies,
I know the murder in a painter's eye
as he reaches for red.
I was the child sent to bed in a prism,
the triangular room under the roof
where a spider blew threads
then walked the visible second of breath.
I saw the sun flattened by his hand,
the clouds stacked like acrobats—
at six my little house of sticks hit by lightning:
one bold stroke, the lash against canvas
alight with my privacy. I watched him come over the hill
lugging thunder in a black case.

I watched him nail a vein for the red river
in *Borneo,*
lift my face for the face of the midget in *Quint,*

stick that fifth-of-an-inch grin of his own
on *Fool's Moon.*
Where it stays to trail me.

He began by assembling clues:
the glass, the telephone and blue soap.
Coaxing the murder that no one saw
from the stubborn evidence of light.

The ventriloquism of color, he said.
Purple and green bleeding through white.
The plum split in the skeleton's hand.
See through the suspension, he said

and I see snow fences, the red skull of sun.
Driving west
the windshield a question of light fielded
left.
Speeding, I see all
he chose for me to see.

Please. Imagine the two of us
out walking in a stubbled field at sunset
watching a fox rise and turn for the woods.
Imagine my cries—for the fox
run down like this to his life.
Knowing how next to me
the fox runs in his eyes
and dies
in a typical nimbus of light.
Imagine my cries in the center of that sight.

Though it appears we are carefree,
in the photograph we look sleepy—

just like any father and daughter
out watching the sun go down.

Ransom

This is a poem of ransom
for the child walking,
her white shoes and sash
growing whiter in the dark

the stars growing white above her.
Stolen by her parents
away from the park
and the safe streets . . .

The child is walking in the dark,
dreaming the baby back in the carriage,
back in the arms of the nurse
and further back

she is dreaming the arms of the star,
the blue poppy. There are carp in the pools.
There are fools everywhere
with parasols and white canes

and she is walking through the dark
with a gun to her head,
through miles of white blindfold.
The car is humming next to the curb,

they are calling her
but she keeps walking. The night is being built
by the architect of darkness in just this way,
exact in every detail to the night she was born . . .

And what does she see, walking?
The dead in the graveyards demanding their elegies,
the blood of the first son on the doorstep,
stars levying tax for their bright insufficiency.

She is saving each white coin of thought
for blood money, for a poem of walking
away, years later, from the man and woman in her mind,
who sit at the kitchen table.

Her shoes are pure white now.
She will keep walking,
the car will stop following, the graveyard
will yield up its few tarnished words

and the poem will begin, years later,
the ransom note written.
She knows this for certain:
she will have herself back.

Choreography

Though most of the time she ignores it,
the city comes at night offering itself
in the abstract, the way you might have imagined
New York for a musical comedy star: a fixture moon,
a corner uptown where dreams stay and radiate.

It is almost night. She turns a corner,
swings her cape—and what remains in the air
is not choreography, but flight, the black wing
vanishing against gravity.

A background drops. She inhabits her body again
and listens to the riveters, the shadow whip
unwinding night, winding her woman's body
in the silk clothes of the assassin.

Somewhere, in a garden of jade, sits Buddha.
He is neither holy nor just
but has been carved from stone in a world
which has invented holiness and justice.

His old motionless dance
she finds most fitting; where, in her mind,
in the folded abstraction of the lotus,
a gesture holds a single radiance.

But like an obsession, a series of dance steps
done over and over to the wrong rhythm,
she insists on it

the surprise backhand motion of thought
evading itself: refusing finally to dance,
to mime the night or the names drawn
on the wallpaper of stone. So she walks alone.
So the riveters of shadow begin again
like the fist pounding the news
into newsprint. To deliver,
folded in abstraction,
the new day.

War Crimes

After a while
in weariness
the body would relinquish
some of its gifts of ingratiation:

the power of muscle to rise slightly above bone
the power to arch the pelvis as in sex
the ability of hands to press air
in gestures of supplication
or tenderness.

And in this reduction,
the body, inevitably,
would grow softer,
more attached to its surroundings,

the eyes taking in the room
its pageant of bad taste
the important masks of the torturers.

And the brain in the body
would imagine the emptiness of this room
in ten years
the intent of wilderness within it,
of rubble,
the rose growing through the grilled transom
above the doorway—

and would feel such pity
and so apart from other men in this sentiment

that the great nerve
which runs from head to pelvis
which makes us courteous
shy
scrupulous
makes us touch one another with gentleness

would tremble
till it was plucked
held in the pliers
then in the fire

shriveling in that little violence
of heat and light

which in another form
we often refer to
as love.

Fireflies

for EDWARD HEALTON

We walked together up that country road.
It was dark. Vermont. Another season.
Then, looking up, we saw the sky explode
with fireflies. Thousands, in one frisson
of cold light, scattered in the trees, ablink
in odd synchrony. That urgency,
that lightening pulse, would make us stop, think
of our own lives. The emergency

that brought us here. The city, separation
and the pain between us. Your hands that heal
can't make us whole again; this nation
of lovestruck bugs can't change that. Still, we feel
the world briefly luminous, the old spark
of nature's love. Around us now, the dark.

Opium

The ant asleep in the poppy
wakes up at the sound, the gunfire
of sun on the wings. Here comes

the Minister of Opium in his plane,
seeing nothing but red fields. Poppies
fall from his hatband and in the city,
the nickel swamis step back into their

doorways predicting: *more storm.* You
can see it coming yourself, the road home
is a detour and you come back to the black
lacquered matchbox on the dash, full of
waving stalks, the plane smoking, circling.

You will see the same things forever: its red
fingernails down the rain's sides, its hand on the wheel
next to your hand. Every truck on the pier

backs up into hindsight—
egged on by the rear-view mirror's hint of being
half of some other thing, some sudden reversal
of all we looked forward to. Say you want your
body back before dawn—then shoulder the rifle,
pick a steel bird backward from the sky with your eye
on that slight differential, your eye on that different

kickback that hauls your arm up twice: once in surprise,
again in a thing that could pass anywhere for that emotion.
Now you're somewhere so anonymous, you could say

I love you to the tree
where your initials, with hers, fit
perfectly into the old heart. The moon
keeps smoothing over everything, shines on
a couple of hubcaps underwater, where once
a driver let the wheel go.

The river forks over a rough ton, two.
And the bottlecaps, the red chime of the ant
on a petal keeps catching up like the headlights
behind you—like this traffic so fast it goes

backward into a starless future, where, no fooling,
you had a real bad accident.

Dream Sheriff

for SUSIE

You say you have a talent for this.
I believe you
the dream sheriff
believes you

but you're under arrest anyway.
Under arrest:
I never told you about
the pine tree
that stopped moving once
when I looked at it

did I

or the night I burst into flames
protesting nature's voyeurism

dream sheriff
let's agree:
here is a room
here is a bed

there are two people here
one in love
the other
unconscious.

II

Poem

There is a world
made entirely of paper,
and when I think
of the little tree of my brain
on its stem

I know what feeds the conflagration.
The sun is uncivilized
and thank god for that.
These debates between the just
and the hungry don't make sense of this:

the percussion of snow,
the bloody cymbals.

But take the bible,
take all the books,
and here is a summary:

the stutter of life on these keys,
the brain's shrub red to the thorns
with thought. In that final hour,
we will stand on our words
for proximity to heaven

and the soul will sit patient
on its stair, telling its
indecipherable alphabet.

Census

Here's how we were counted:
firstborn, nay-sayers,
veterans, slow-payers,
seditionists, convicts,
half-breeds, has-beens,
the nearly defined dead,
all the disenfranchised live.

Once everybody had a place
among the nameless. Now we
can't afford to be anonymous.

Consider, they said, the poor,
the misfit—consider the woman
figuring herself per cent.

Consider the P.A. system making
a point so intimate I petition
not to be anybody's good guess
or estimate. I ask to be one:

maybe widow-to-be watching the sun
diminish brick by brick along the jail
wall and also that green pear
on its drunken roll out
of the executioner's lunch basket.
At 12:01, 02, in the cocked chamber
of the digital clock
the newsman said: *There'll be less*

work in the new century. And my job
will be, as usual, forgetting—
or getting it backwards—

each non-integer, tender and separate,
fake rosebud, Rolodex, cab full of amputees
obedient to traffic, moss on the baby's headstone . . .

minus and minus' shock each minute,
the kiss, its loss,
each newborn and condemned-to-be
in one breath executed, and blessed.

Her Story: Leaving Eden

She knew whose idea death was.
It had been *river* and *wind*
until she turned her back
in the blue depot of reeds
where she bathed,
understanding at last
the relationship of skin to bone.

The first day he swung an ax: the sun fell.
The second, she saw the fire's brand on his body,
the debt he would exact
son to son
into her gratitude.
Now the harlot could plait her hair into history.
Now the dead could invent the hourglass.

So God was improvident,
his right arm an abomination of prophecy.
She could have prophesied
the writ of the lily,
the rise of the tribe of instinct.
She could have prophesied you,
in the thousands of generations,
in the dead city, with your woman-hair gone wild.
You, with your slogan-mouth,
your shoulders opening at the intersection
of heart and armor. You.

But she did not prophesy.
In the moon,
in the shadow of the mandible,
she said nothing.
She sowed her illiterate grain.
The womb was all she knew of the future—
her only prophecy—
and even that, o my sisters,
in a language we have yet to translate.

Cheap Scent

Garters lying like pale insects
on her thighs
and jazz, ephemeral, familiar,
roses floating in a bowl.
The moment fills with birds
and she becomes sure of the music
as a habit of plumage,
a silk dress she wears to death.

She lets him cross a carpet,
lets him touch her face

and later
a lake:
indistinct dancing.

And later,
shaking out her hair,
she touches the soft trammeled planet
of the atomizer, blowing cheap scent
in the air
              where it remains
like an excessive gesture. He says
she could be blind from the side,
a white craving presses against her profile.
White Shoulders. Toujours Moi.

She walks all the way back,
rain drowns in a gutter

falling down to the lake
far below her shoes.

A garter in her mind
presses hard against a metal chair,
a bare leg,
and lingers there

as tenderness,
unmentionable pain.

Short Histories of the Sea

I

The shape of a boat
suggested itself
from the idea

of sea as surface.
What was beneath
had nothing to do with history

as they invented it:
sailor
warrior
king.

Only the figure
on the bowsprit
stared down blue corridors
to the past.

The octopus
with her slow conceptual waltz,
her grasping motion
refined later into fingers:
in the sea
she is historian.

Everyday a lamprey
bows to a tree of seaweed.

It bows back.
Two centuries pass.
This is an historical movement.

Above, we've never learned very well
what makes us famous—
the past turning up
in the genes
spontaneously

with nothing to say
about loving ourselves
as fish
or feminine gesture

and no mention
of this other history writing itself
in the body's tides
in spite of us.

In spite of us:
the blood's armor tightening,
the wing unfurling at the temple.

II

They came into the harbor
on a day much like this
at six
they stood on the decks
congratulating each other
crying So this is Carthage

and sailed past
the monuments to Artemis

threw coins
calling O Tyre O Sidon

and beside them historians
wrote poems
in which
the sea was an eccentric
tempestuous character

and plants below
the bearded surface
grew huge
with a sweet morphic odor

much like the scent of roses
we know on earth.

Chivalry

In Benares
the holiest city on earth
I saw an old man
toiling up the stone steps
to the ghat
his dead wife in his arms
shrunken to the size
of a child—
lashed to a stretcher.

The sky filled with crows.
He held her up for a moment
then placed her
in the flames.

In my time on earth
I have seen few acts of true chivalry
or reverence
of man for woman.

But the memory of him
with her
in the cradle of his arms
placing her just so in the fire
so she would burn faster
so the kindling of the stretcher
would catch—

is enough for me now,
will suffice
for what remains on this earth
a gesture of bereavement
in the familiar carnage of love.

Ahimsa

Say you walked in the shadowy garden
in Amritsar, before night descended,
tried to imagine the massacre, that crazy saint
Gandhi and the people on their knees to a god
less civilized than he. You would disagree, agree . . .
violence teaches nothing.

Violence teaches nothing.
The violence of nature, the empty garden,
famine and drought, we agree,
teach nothing. But the British rifles descending
slightly in the angle of fire, aiming at God
in the bodies beneath them, aiming at the saints . . .

teach that man's violence is different. The saint
himself had an inclination to punish for nothing,
hated the body in the familiar way of all mystics. God
would not judge the dead in that garden.
It was the Mahatma, descended
from sin as he saw it, who always agreed

to let the body die for higher cause. Agree
or disagree, *ahimsa* implies saint
and the rest, for mankind, is a descended
set of values. Nothing
prepares us for our own heroism. The garden
that day held bodies ten deep. God

said nothing. Gandhi took the place of God.
Ahimsa is another way to disagree.
Say you walked in the shadowy garden
in Amritsar, wondering what it takes to be a saint.
To love perfection, scorn the flesh. Nothing
in common with the man who descended

to his wife as the soul descends
into hell. If you did look for God
in the body—it would teach nothing
but provide grounds to agree:
the skin, the hands, the sainted
navel. Would you die in this garden?

Night descends. Disagree, agree.
The children of Amritsar are godless, forget the saint.
Nothing remains but the same questions, flowers in the garden.

Real Estate

You think you earned this space on earth,
but look at the gold face of the teen-age
pharaoh, smug as a Shriner, in his box

with no diploma, a plot flashy enough
for Manhattan. Early death, then what
a task dragging a sofa into the grave,
a couple of floor lamps, the alarm set

for another century. Someday we'll heed
the testament of that paid escort watching
himself in all the ballroom mirrors: slide

with each slide of the old trombone,
be good to the bald, press up against
the ugly duck-like. Time is never old,

never lies. What a past you'd have
if you'd only admit to it: the real estate
your family dabbled in for generations,
the vacant lots developed like the clan

overbite—through years of sudden
foreclosure. Who knows what it costs?
First you stand for the national anthem,

then you start waltzing around without
strings, reminding yourself of yourself,

expecting to live in that big city
against daddy's admonition: buy land

get some roots down under those spike
heels, let the river bow and scrape as
it enters the big front door of your property.

Golden Retriever

She was the one who put her tongue
to the whetstone on its rickety wheel
in the Tool Room. The wheel spun,
the tongue arched in its bud and bent

against that dizzy syllable of grit.
Still she could never say what she meant.
When she had her tenth birthday cake
that winter, she stuttered her thanks for

the new blades, skated backward on the rink
into a room holding the sunset. The snow was falling
in it, unstoppered, odorless as chloroform.
Under the x'ed surface of the ice hung

a gold tuft from the day her brother flooded
and made the retriever sit in the wet as it
hardened. He was a pup then, but was trained to obey.
It made him mean, doing what anyone said to do,

but he did it all the same. Down in the rec
room, she pushed 12 on the Rock-Ola and the
records wobbled on their neon stalk, the red
planets circled each other inside the glass.

It was a room for fun, they said, and though
it was, it still lit up with loss, the kind that
comes from debts collected. Or so she imagined—
piano and pool table: odd courtesies of foreclosure.

On the polished bar a lit triptych said *Hamm's*
Beer, its waterfall of blue tinsel rippling behind
the beaver paddling a canoe up front. *The retriever,*
trained to hunt, would point for minutes at a dying

bird, then fetch whatever you sent him for—till
he bit a neighbor's child who touched his unhealed sore.
What happened happened. No cause and effect connected
her tongue and her troubled heart and never would. The pain

came on its own and pointed for minutes at whatever
was wounded before her. In the end, she might have
to break its neck, because of that pain. Maybe
she imagined a family on the edge of a windy precipice

and—just like that, retrieved them as she stood at
the opened door of the jukebox, sliding in a few new
disks for her dad. Maybe she could bring back his hand
on her shoulder as they stood staring into the glass

juke singing "Rock Island Line." *A bird hurt bad*
will wing-limp for acres to save itself. She knew
even then it was better to be dead than weaponed
in her way and laid down like a ragged prize
at the foot of his dream, his least sufficiency.

Women's House

Sometimes I go willingly to prison,
slip in through the gate, open nights
for the late bails, the midnight shift.
I don't work here. I only report the talk.
Bucky, for example, wants to be a man,
get a pelican lawyer* to plead sex change.

Bucky claims a little change
can't hurt, wants to try prison
from the inside of an outsider, a man.
Personally, I come here to feel at home. All night
a hooker sits with the D.A., not refusing to talk,
refusing to admit she's a man—and what shiftless

convictable john can prove not? Double up on the night shift
is the motto here. A suspect changes
clothes, not inclination. Juanita talks
like a lady to a lady prisoner
who cut her baby up. Night struts in with night:
in a sequined dress, in tits, in the body of a man,

a woman. This is the Women's House, just as men
imagine it. And here, her silver shift
slit to god's shaved crotch, is the woman. Pimp gone, night
riding her heels. I used to say to myself, *change
white girl. Be black. Be Bucky, her prison
wife, Juanita.* Maybe I thought I'd talk

* Appellate lawyer

different. Maybe I thought I'd be talk's
best whore: like, tie a necktie, be a man—
undo it, a woman. God, every body's a prison
in the Dept. of Correction, graveyard shift.
A human hand touches one of us and we change,
we can't say how: call it sex, the night,

our own bad upbringing. Criminal and night
guard sit, wrist over wrist, in a coffin of desultory talk,
handcuffed to each other. Bucky wants to call Dr. Change,
collect. The D.A.'s had it, says, "Bitch, man
or woman?" The ironic ranks, unclassified at the last shift,
stretch from here to dawn, we prisoners.

Chasers

India, 1973

If there'd been a moon, it might have restored
illusion: our usual point of view. It might
have whitewashed the temples, the skeletal
bodies of the boatmen. But it was almost light
when the drowned rose, clairvoyant, around us—
we saw them float, indifferent to the brain's
civility, its shocked panning for gold.
It was dawn. The boatmen stuck poles
in the red mud and where the famous current
reverses itself, they sweated and cursed
our tourist souls. When the skiff touched shore,
we rose and single-filed through stone
to the ghats, where the newly dead burned
effortlessly, in that other present.

*

Past the kiosks in Chandi Chowk, in an upstairs
room in Hari Bali Street, the perfume merchants
touch the dead woman, here, there, with vetivert,
attar of rose . . . preparing her to float in air.
The beggars in the street sell their dreams:
the dream of the anointed limbs, the blessing
of the new bride in her gold sari. Back at the hotel,
the starving crooner lip-synchs into his mike.
You drink and I dream the dream I purchased:
upstairs in Chandi Chowk the body in its gold sari

leaves the embalming table, the forbidden oils,
floats back into the beggar's sleep, asking for the pyre,
the flaming oven—anything but this grave of air,
this soul selling itself into the dreams of another.

*

The moon's on trial in its own courtroom:
where did this woman come from, drunk near the pool,
unrolling her stockings, kicking off her shoes,
wading into the shallowest part? She interrogates
her cocktail, she names names. In the bar,
behind a screen, a turbaned man in a band jacket
lifts his horn. *Tenderly.* Closer up, the two of us
sit in the mirror's reflection, a candle burning
down between us, a stump of amputated flame.
The biscuits half-risen in the oven collapse
in time for our dinner. The goddess raises her many arms.
The mirror turns iridescent.
The moon rolls over, guilty, guilty again.

*

When the visitors ascend,
(as in their idea of the natural order),
they rise in glass elevators,
with leather suitcases, and the Hotel Karma
prepares to serve them, happy to procure
whatever they least desire. Would the guests
prefer bedside light, *eau de minerale,*
refrigerated wind? The guests will have spirit
lamps, broken adaptors, the Untouchables outside
their doors—waiting to sweep the rooms
with their brooms of fire, waiting to open
the heavy dark curtains to pain, obsession,
the malarial insects of the night.

*

In a trader mood, you visit me,
Polo to my walled state, my ringed city
of spite. The ability of the female
to withstand persuasion is legendary,
like Shalimar, those gardens built
by one lover for another in shapes
of perfect neurosis. When they lay
together under the alabaster fountain,
the trained birds sang with minor passion.
It was clear from the architecture:
she did not love him.

*

The goddess lifts her many arms.
I think of harvest—
how a God might say that Heaven
already relinquishes too much to us:
good soil, pain medication. Even love,
now that the guesswork's gone.
But adoration is small, love's chaser,
love's thanks. I find myself praying
to salt, to the slamming door.
She was there all the time,
not so much to be worshipped,
but as a kind of vision—
making us paint the same landscape
again and again till we began to see it.
She lifted her arms and there was a bed
to sleep in, fruit on the table,
the mirror, as in India, on fire.

III

Skylight

Take my best friend up to your rooms,
show her the paintings, the woman's face
laughing at nothing but the tattoo
of a heart on a part of the body we hide.

Show her the books, the way
scent unwinds from the syllable
of incense.

But save till last
the place that came to me
afterward so often in my dreams—
the steps leading up,
the ending in sky.

And in dreams, for nights at a time,
I would imagine finding a few stars
I could stand on, facing north
into the world of the poor.

Let her see the view last,
the sky light, so that she can imagine
architecture,
a literature that dissolves into air.

I know the world is full of happy people,
the obliging poor of your world tour,
who loved listening to you
standing in sun in their tired skins
with their best friends, their little property.

But what would the government do
with a world this familiar?
Where would the empire extend itself
if the poor forfeited their imagination?

The greenhouse reels in its glass capacity,
the flora inside diminished in fact.
Ex-friend, there's an elevator
that never stops rising,

there's a house hung in the sky
where you sit with my best friend,
my umbrella full of holes.

Everyday now I go into my life
where, often, it's raining
and the night's as small as a pair of hands.

I have found comfort lately
in the notion of gravity,
how the bread stays on the blue plate,
how my best friend places weight on one foot,
walking.

All that is the gift of limit
and beyond it is the scaffold of passion
beyond it is the sky
to which I had right
all that time.

Chapter One

You said it over the top of the book,
you said it softly: *No no*

in disbelief, the way the heroine cries
No in a later chapter, as it dawns on her
who she is and why she is in this book.

And the novel left open to the murder scene
lets the murder scene be altered gradually
by the light from the window—so the killer
will bring the ax down on her skull

against the light blue sky forming at the edge
of the page. Never again will print betray you
like this. Never again will your hands travel
with hers along the blind margins, grasp

the gunwales of the invented rowboat, gather
the oars like crutches, limping up the black pond
into another plot. *It will be sunny all day today.*

It will be sunny tomorrow. I can't go anywhere
unless someone writes it first. Everyday I dust,
and my mother shoves the Hoover around in a huff.
Like her, I have someone dying on my hands and

the sun sits completely down on the coffee table,
on a crystal ball with a wax rose inside that refuses
to close or open all the way. I can write it now:

how the rising dust occurred to me like the
thought of crime, how I didn't expect to be
forgiven as I picked it up and shook the sleeping
hurricane. So slowly at first my mother didn't notice

the wax rose blowing authorless away from the dustcloth,
the unchristened bitch rising up chapter by chapter
to throw it all out: the ending, the beginning,
the unwrit heavens already opening to receive her.

Tuesday Again

Morning starts a shallow machinery
in my skull. It's Tuesday.
Outside the same unskilled bird
begins a chorus of mistakes.
I'd kill him
if guilt weren't a factor here.

If I had heavier shades,
a dark parchment morning couldn't pierce,
I would have to invent another form
of suffering
to take up the slack
before the cold bathtub.

See, everything justifies itself in the end.
On one hand, life's more literal,
you get dream analysis,
a textbook of survival.

On the other,
secret vulgarity!
Fox in the closet,
the fur you sleep under.

No one understands it,
the lust of Siberians.

No one ever notices
my sled on the edge of the precipice,

this dream I've had for weeks now
of wingprints in the snow.

Special Delivery to Curtis:
The Future of the World

The sky over Cyprus is blue and usual. And you want me to move there for politics. Believe me, the sky over Manhattan is white. Everyday the same parade passes on Fifth Avenue.

And even if we could demonstrate, join hands as far downtown as that last bar, our lives would not try convention.

What women we are! One drink and the radio's topical nonsense makes sense, the way destiny appeals to the hopeless. That's politics.

And I take no pride in circumstance. There's an ambitious biography writing itself in my future having to do with the dirty white proscenium of the park and the occasion it frames: two women, a traffic light stuck on red.

I'm a feminist. There are the lives we need to survive and those we don't. Of course, everyone loves a crippled debutante. Everyone loves a calendar. Did you say it was Wednesday? *I'm a feminist.* Don't take that chair, we're expecting a feminist. Is there life after rhetoric?

No. Just this moment. Two women. The future of the world. And this poor light holding the only crown it owns over your incomparable profile, the brilliant manifesto of your hair.

Par

I knew the course
the way a mole knows traffic.
Trudging across the green
thinking formally,
coldly,
I hate clover. I love clover.

How should I know what was bothering me?
It was hot.
There were links:
the sprinkler's self-deprecating gestures,
a patch of mint,
the pocked skin of a golf ball.

I had new breasts,
a big ponytail grew from the back of my head
like a question mark.

Under the pure surface of the fairway
the mole swam
in his dark harness
and I sat

faintly surprised by myself,
by the flat horizon. Nowhere to hide the body!
Nowhere the sun could sink
without being seen.

In my modest colloquial speech:
the sun rises. The sun sets.
It is Wednesday
and that command issued
in their semi-military tongue
must mean *Move it*.
My answer translated freely,
would be something like:
Tee off in the freezer

and still we obscure
the thrust of the verb
heading west toward my thought process.

Here's how I choose to remember it:
it is summer
in the local sahara . . .
I am at half-mast
in a sand trap
trying to arrange myself
in the space of time it takes
someone to say
I love you.

And then they're screaming it
FORE! FORE!
and we're lying there
exposed to
the sun
the rough

someone else's bad idea
of a good sport.

Idolatry

for DELMIRA AGUSTINI
(1880–1914)

You wrote: "it would be no better to hold God's head
in your hands." That was before you knew
God wore a horse trader's suit
and came strutting through Pocitos,
looking over the shoulders of the locals:

the dimsighted, the skittish,
the dray nag in tandem with the graveyard plug.
The world, in his image, bored him
till he heard you talking. Every groan
or curse surfaced to him as prayer

and even the makeshift heresy of language
meant less to him than gesture, the gold
in the trough raised to power.
That little doll you carried—he figured
you worshipped it—though you worshipped just

its invention: nails and hint of teeth,
its wheeze of puppet lust. Idolatry
was that small—but you could pray
to the prayer itself, word after word
on the rolling pedestals. Dear Jesus,

the curtains don't live up to it,
the china pitcher, the mantilla,

the rosary nor candles lit to the dead—
don't live up. When you crossed your heart
and put your head down, you saw the veins

bulge in the studded livery,
his glove full of blood on your body
and on this very night he begged you to love him,
he begged you, already counting your ribs
and the proud occipital bones.

He was God, a horse trader, and he didn't think
it would take but a month
to break you.

Coincidence

for TOM

What a coincidence. The color of our hair.
Ancestral blood. You arriving as I do,
our arrival in light. Shine up the pyres now,
we can see clear through to the past:
one big erasure on the map of Europe.
What a common hospitality: a tongue.

For example, this dumb lullaby we speak.
The crooked hem of language
grazing our lips in sleep and sleep's
incandescent syllables
that become the day's predictable grammar.

How can I say it in speech—
that I remember you
like the first extension of myself
in sunlight? The first touch.
And further back. The beginning of the body
in other bodies, the hall of mirrors
from which we are borne.

I believe that we are born extending ourselves
and except for death's different fingerprints
on our flesh, I'd say this love's incestuous;

except for the mind's inscape,
I'd blame the same birth-star, the beginning,
which falls and divides, eyelash by eyelash,
improbable as luck, love's coincident.

Elocution: Touch

When you touch me,
I recover.

It's a miracle.
A simple, well-lit situation
in which there are two people,
a bed,

a memory
I can't describe.
So here is a metaphor:
a child who stammers.

And here is fear,
a synaptical whip
lashing thought ahead of the stuttering tongue.
So the child can't ever say it,

can't name the thing
he sees
or puts his hand on—
mouth
darkness
heart.

Think of the state
where the tongue leans
against the roof of the mouth

and loves the shape of every syllable
freed from the uvular space

where the white nerve lightning
stops long enough to let
the tunnel intend one breath, articulate,

so the child can
all at once
say it

the word I remembered
when you placed your hands
on my skin.
When you said something
and I answered you
effortlessly

in another language: the one
I was born speaking.

The Fault

for LYNNE MCMAHON
and SHEROD SANTOS

I

At dawn, falling asleep on the freeway,
I watch the sun come up in purgatory
and pray with the radio: *Save us.*
Past nuclear reactors, the blind remainders

of the brain: *Save us.* L.A. to Newport,
the eye becomes its own compass: due south
is the globe's curve, not Hell, though
the earth lowers and extends: one enormous runway
into the mouth of the diamond mine. The aerial

tows a light, the hood lamps pick a hitchhiker,
offramp. The searchlights tangle in ice plant, climbing the exit
wall. The burning eyelids of the savior move
on a marquee. . . . The News reports it's snowing again

Back East, though I can't imagine that kind of white.
The day I learned to swim, there were no clouds,
just the dissolving monument of sand and I sank
without sound, where the reef dropped like a fault

in the earth and perched a long time on the gravestones
before surfacing. Then I swam, that simple ambivalent
stroke beginners use, with no faith in the body's buoyancy,

no faith in the oldest fault,
the parched intelligence of tide.

II

What is the name of that flower?

The wind sidesteps itself
in the courtyard
where the lame learn the waltz of the crutch.
Bougainvillea. Mimosa.

I have use for the gratuitous;
spurs dragging in dust,
a turn in death's rented tux.
This could be a hospital in paradise—

nothing shines all night like these bedside iris,
nothing shines like the feet of the dying.
I swear I have roots somewhere.
I've learned to stand perfectly still
and fill the flower with my anxieties.
Narcissus. Forsythia.

I've learned to applaud the dervish palms,
the deaf. This may not be summer,
but the wind's in the cyclamen.
Imagine a word that specific.

Imagine a skidmark, a dazzling limp
across the continent between our hearts.
There are purple flowers
along this road
and the earth laid out on its altar
has no last words for us.

It's light again
and again I sign love,
my imaginary name.

IRVINE, CALIF.
WINTER, 1978

Androgyny

So you woke up holding it—
the aura of possession
which surrounds a single thought.
Not apperception,
a halo, an obsession.

You couldn't comb your hair
without turning to stone.
You were imagining it
even under the plumbing: water steaming up
your glassed-in skeleton.

With his hands between your legs
you dreamed the gold wings of the parenthesis

and saw the lenses of his eyes
as center of the afterthought—

but you were wrong. And wrong
to love the sun's blunt
easing in through the screen.
They beat you because you let them.

But seeing him in the parenthesis of sun,
in the gold of the museum
you thought: she is my brother

and you saw the dream physiognomy,
the dream muscles, the whole new breath.

And you were right
and you didn't know it

as no near-human, womb consciousness
ever knows the moment before
it is about
to be.

SIREN SONGS

SIREN SONGS

The Funeral

We went down to the ocean, wearing
the silk hats we wore to the funeral.
It was like a party, people drank
too much. No one mentioned the dead
child. Someone said that the idea for
escalators came from the waves.
A woman interpreted dreams: a window
stood for fear, a wheatfield, fate.
I lay down and dreamed that I was on
an escalator traveling rapidly through
a window into a wheatfield. She said
I was afraid, I was efficient, I was
doomed. I said she was humorless.
But we were sad and overtaken by it:
nothing to watch out there but
the escalators, the wheatfields,
the child learning to swim through
the thousands of sunlit windows.

SIREN SONGS

Friend on Stilts

Stilts
sink into stiltprints
left by the dead child in the soft earth.

If his living friend stalks in those holes,
if he throws each long crutch stiff-legged
ahead of him, will he win the race?
One dead foot, one live . . . he hops on bones,
a lame pony, a giraffe limping fast till it falls.

At the burial, everyone looks up
as he nears. From great height, he plucks
a shoulder-high blossom, drops it—
letting it drift down into the dirt rowboat

under the trees. The grass shudders
against his wooden shins. He begins
his descent, picking his way to the grave.

SIREN SONGS

Dulce lignum, dulces clavos

He watched everything from his cross. At six, I was already eager to help, to distract myself from his gaze, washing the chalk words from the blackboard. After school, I stood on a stool to reach the high sink and turn the black wheels of the faucets. I looked out the window as the pail filled. I saw the boy looking up at me and instantly I was in the middle of a crowd in the street below and he was dead, lying there. The nun bent down and turned my head away, pressed it against her breast, the cold metal crucifix. Her heart beat inside my head. When I stole a glance, I saw how he lay on the rusty cowcatcher, staring at me with the same calculated expression, a kind of dare.

Today someone asked, *Were there still streetcars in 1952?* But that's just it, it doesn't matter: she was holding me against her, I had to invent circumstances in order to see at all. Then, for one second, I understood everything: the chalk letters, the nails, her arms around me, why he had to die for us.

SIREN SONGS

Emergency

I think the hill feeds him. He dreams the way he once dreamed
in bed, but he is trying harder: the hill is growing smaller, a
nearly formed thought. Like the sky. No one else believes that he
is coming back. All night the light shines from the city hospital
into the heavens—the emergencies. When he tries to think again,
the light will gather under his headstone. Not enough to read by.
Or write. The marble angel stares back at me with the exact look
of startled perfection the Virgin saw that morning. He must have
been as embarrassed as she was—finding himself inside that pas-
sionate boy's body, holding himself motionless at the doorway
till she would envision wings. She stood in the garden, clear-
eyed, smiling. But in order to make her believe, he had to repeat
the message over and over, resummoning his little human
speech. He wanted to touch her as she listened, calmed by his
flattery, but he restrained himself . . . knowing how easily they
trust, then are given over unto death.

Carol Muske was born in St. Paul, Minnesota. In 1970 she earned an M.A. in Creative Writing at the State University of California-San Francisco. Her first book of poems, CAMOUFLAGE, was published by The University of Pittsburgh Press. She currently teaches in the M.F.A. Writing Program at Columbia, is the Director of Art Without Walls, and is a Jenny McKean Moore Lecturer at George Washington University.